Please Come for Dinner

12 Easy & Elegant Menus for Busy Cooks

Pat Ross

Art by Carolyn Bucha

Time-Life Books
Alexandria, Virginia

Time-Life Books is a division of Time Life Inc.
President & CEO : George Artandi

Time-Life Books
President: Stephen R. Frary

Time-Life Custom Publishing
Vice President and Publisher: Terry Newell
Vice President of Sales and Marketing: Neil Levin
Vice President, Acquisitions & Executive Editor: Kate Sheehan Hartson
Director of Special Sales: Liz Ziehl
Project Manager: Jennifer M. Lee
Production Manager: Carolyn Clark
Quality Assurance Manager: James D. King

Printed and bound in China

Library of Congress Cataloging-in-Publication Data
Ross, Pat, 1943-
Please Come for Dinner: 12 Easy & Elegant Menus for Busy Cooks /Pat Ross:
art by Carolyn Bucha.
p. cm.
ISBN: 0-7835-5308-0
I. Dinners and dining. 2. Menus. I. Title.
TX737.R65   1998
642'.4—dc2I   97-4291I
CIP

Books produced by Time-Life Custom Publishing are available at special bulk
discount for promotional and premium use. Custom adaptations can also be created
to meet your specific marketing goals. Call 1-800-323-5255.

WITH THANKS TO MY EDITOR KATE HARTSON
AND ALL THE SMART AND ENTHUSIASTIC
PEOPLE AT TIME-LIFE BOOKS—JENNIFER
LEE, DONIA STEELE, AND LIZ ZIEHL AMONG THEM—FOR
THEIR SUPPORT. MANY WONDERFUL RECIPE SUGGESTIONS
MADE THEIR WAY INTO THIS COOKBOOK. PETER MIRABELLA,
MY FRIEND AND THE OWNER OF THE POPULAR DANTE'S IN
NEW YORK CITY, AND HIS CHEF LOUISE MUNOZ, ARE
CERTAINLY AT THE TOP OF MY LIST. APPRECIATION ALSO TO
SUSAN QUICK WHO GAVE THIS BOOK HER CREATIVE
TOUCH. LAST BUT NOT LEAST, KEN'S WELL-PLANNED
KITCHEN MADE TESTING THE RECIPES A JOY. HE GETS THE
CLEAN PLATE AWARD PLUS MY LOVE AND THANKS FOR
ALWAYS DOING THE DISHES.

Menus

HOW TO BE A GUEST AT YOUR OWN DINNER PARTY

When it comes to having friends for dinner, most of us are long on intentions and invariably short on time, space, and help when the night arrives. This user-friendly cookbook was designed for the busy person who enjoys entertaining with a memorable home-cooked meal, but has little inclination to fuss over complicated preparations or the serving of endless courses.

Here are 12 perfect menus featuring delicious dishes that go well together. Whether the meal is to be a romantic dinner for two, a stovetop supper for eight, or a buffet for a crowd, there's an emphasis on seasonal foods and fresh herbs. It's amazing what a snip of fresh dill, a pinch of ground nutmeg, or a splash of good olive oil can do. These elegant yet surprisingly simple recipes offer step-by-step directions, and there are thoughtful suggestions for preparing dishes—or portions of dishes—in advance. For example, the rich tomato broth for the Hearty Seafood Soup can be made the day before; and the spicy Cajun-Style Meat Loaf with Salsa can be made weeks in advance and frozen. A main course such as the Burgundy Pot Roast with Vegetables & Potatoes is happy to wait on the stove until you're ready to heat and serve.

The idea is to be a guest at your own dinner party—not a drudge in the kitchen. So *Please Come for Dinner* makes time *in* the kitchen faster and easier by favoring popular and healthy dishes that may be served hot or at room temperature, or that are easily reheated in a microwave oven. Since quality always pleases over quantity, guests will long remember the tastiness of the dish over the number of the dishes served. With that in mind, *Please Come for Dinner* makes life easier with well-balanced menus appropriate for a variety of occasions. Casual or formal, indoors or alfresco, here is a harmony of dishes that will assure a perfect evening.

Many menus come with a suggestion for a bread or rolls—from peasant bread to corn muffins. With so many fine baked breads at the local market, most busy people simply prefer to buy the bread. When it comes to an easy, light, and welcome finish to the meal, a fresh seasonal fruit recipe is the dessert of choice. Beloved Brownies, Snappy Apple Crisp, and Old-Fashioned Gingerbread take into consideration those with a sweet tooth.

Maybe it's time you treated yourself to an evening at home with friends. Invite them for dinner!

YEAR-ROUND FAVORITES

*While the tantalizing aroma of savory herbs and garlic drifts
from the kitchen, relax and enjoy the company of your guests.
This easy meal can be quickly prepared at the end of a busy day.
For a simple first course, serve a lightly dressed salad of baby
greens with sourdough bread. You can make the Glazed &
Tipsy Amaretto Cake the day before because this moist
cake tastes even better the next day.*

GARLIC & HERB ROASTED WHOLE CHICKEN
WITH NEW POTATOES

LEMON DILL BABY CARROTS

GLAZED & TIPSY AMARETTO CAKE

GARLIC & HERB ROASTED WHOLE CHICKEN WITH NEW POTATOES

This amazingly simple whole roasted chicken looks impressive served on a large platter surrounded by the potatoes and garnished with sprigs of fresh parsley and herbs.

Pat dry ONE WHOLE CHICKEN (about 5 POUNDS) with paper towels and place in large roasting pan. Rub skin with 4-5 GARLIC CLOVES crushed. Rub chicken with 2-3 TABLESPOONS OLIVE OIL and the juice of 1 LEMON. Toss juiced lemon into cavity. Sprinkle with 2 TABLESPOONS DRIED THYME, ROSEMARY (crush with your fingers before adding), and MARJORAM. Sprinkle with SALT and FRESHLY GROUND BLACK PEPPER to taste. Roast in 375°F oven for approximately 45 minutes, basting with pan juices once or twice. While chicken is roasting, scrub 12-14 MEDIUM NEW POTATOES and cut in half. Toss potatoes lightly with OLIVE OIL. After the chicken has roasted for 45 minutes, remove from the oven and place the potatoes cut side down around the chicken. Continue cooking for another 30 minutes, or until potatoes are tender and juices run clear when chicken is pierced with a fork.

COOKING TIP:
Before you rub the crushed garlic, lemon, herbs, and olive oil over the chicken, slip a small plastic sandwich bag over your hand for protection.

Serves 4-6

LEMON DILL BABY CARROTS

Many grocery stores make the cook's life easier by carrying prepackaged fresh baby carrots, cleaned and ready.

Steam BABY CARROTS in salted boiling water. (Do not overcook.) Drain water from carrots. Return to pan. Add enough UNSALTED BUTTER to coat carrots. Add Chopped FRESH DILL and SALT and FRESHLY GROUND BLACK PEPPER to taste.

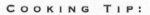

COOKING TIP:
If you wish to prepare this dish an hour or so in advance, run the carrots under cold water
so they don't become too soft, then reheat in microwave just before serving

Serves 4-6

GLAZED & TIPSY AMARETTO CAKE

It's not considered "cheating" to use a prepared cake mix as a base when the results taste like homemade and the time saved is significant. Chill the cake overnight for the best flavor results. The leftover sauce is delicious on ice cream.

Mix together in large mixing bowl: 1 PACKAGE YELLOW CAKE MIX, 1 SMALL PACKAGE INSTANT VANILLA PUDDING, 4 EGGS lightly beaten, ½ CUP COLD WATER, ½ CUP AMARETTO LIQUEUR (or dark rum), and ½ CUP VEGETABLE OIL. Beat with electric mixer for 5 minutes until ingredients are incorporated. Grease a large Bundt pan liberally with butter. Coat the sides and bottom of the pan with ½ CUP FINELY CHOPPED ALMONDS that have been lightly toasted before chopping. Pour in batter. Bake from 1 hour to 75 minutes at 350°F. Cool cake in pan completely before turning out onto a serving plate. Make sauce.

Serves 6-8

AMARETTO SAUCE

Bring the following ingredients to a boil in a small saucepan: 1 CUP DARK BROWN SUGAR, 1 STICK BUTTER, ½ CUP AMARETTO LIQUEUR (or dark rum), and ¼ CUP WATER. Boil for 1 minute. Cool slightly and drizzle half of sauce over cooled cake. Reserve remaining sauce for another use or serve on the side with ice cream.

COOKING TIP:
An electric chopper or coffee grinder is useful when chopping nuts finely.

Serves 6-8 with leftovers

STOVETOP SUPPER

A "stovetop supper" invites guests into the kitchen to line up and ladle this hearty meal right from the pan. Serve with a crusty bread for soaking up the delicious juices. The Lime Cucumber Mousse with Walnuts tastes refreshing and adds a unique texture to the meal. Serve the bread pudding warm.

BURGUNDY POT ROAST WITH VEGETABLES & POTATOES

LIME CUCUMBER MOUSSE WITH WALNUTS

HASTY BLUEBERRY & APRICOT BREAD PUDDING

BURGUNDY POT ROAST WITH
VEGETABLES & POTATOES

Served hot in deep plates or shallow bowls, a savory roast is a complete one-pot meal. Peter Mirabella, owner of Dante's, the New York gourmet shop, says this richly satisfying version is a nightly favorite.

Coat a 4-POUND BEEF ROAST (such as bottom round or brisket) generously on all sides with SALT, FRESHLY GROUND BLACK PEPPER, and PAPRIKA. Heat ¼ CUP VEGETABLE OIL in a large heavy pot with a lid or Dutch oven over high heat. Sear roast on both sides, then remove from pot and set aside. Add another ¼ CUP VEGETABLE OIL to pot. Add 4 GARLIC CLOVES chopped and 2 LARGE ONIONS cut into thick wedges. Sauté until just wilted. Add 4 CARROTS and 4 STALKS CELERY cut into large pieces. Return browned roast to pot and arrange vegetables around it. Add to pot: 4 CUPS CHICKEN BROTH, 1 CUP BURGUNDY WINE (or any dry red wine), ¼ CUP WORCESTERSHIRE SAUCE,

and ONE 14-OUNCE CAN WHOLE PEELED TOMATOES WITH JUICE (crush tomatoes slightly before adding to pot). Bring to a boil, lower heat, and cover pot tightly. Simmer 2-3 hours. Add water if more liquid is needed during cooking. After 1 hour and 30 minutes of cooking, add 6-8 LARGE NEW POTATOES quartered (or 20 small) to pot. Bury potatoes in juice and continue cooking until roast is tender and potatoes are still firm. Before serving, carve roast into thin slices and place back in pot, covering with juices. Add SALT and FRESHLY GROUND BLACK PEPPER to taste. Garnish with sprigs of FRESH ROSEMARY, THYME, or PARSLEY.

COOKING TIP:

If you prefer a thicker gravy, stir in a small amount of cornstarch or flour mixed with water. This should be done before sliced pot roast is returned to the pot.

Serves 6 - 8

LIME CUCUMBER MOUSSE
WITH WALNUTS

The combination of lime gelatin and cottage cheese makes a mousse that is unusual and refreshingly delicious. Serve on tender Bibb lettuce leaves.

Dissolve 1 PACKAGE LIME GELATIN MIX in 1 CUP BOILING WATER. Cool to room temperature. Combine gelatin mixture with 1 CUP COTTAGE CHEESE, 1 CUP MAYONNAISE, 1 CUP PECANS, and 1 MEDIUM CUCUMBER peeled, seeds scooped out, and sliced into large pieces. Pour into a blender or food processor and mix until cucumber and nuts are chopped fine. Pour into a mold and chill. Just before serving, unmold on circle of BIBB LETTUCE LEAVES arranged on a platter.

COOKING TIP:
A plastic gelatin mold with a removable bottom that releases the molded gelatin onto a plate is foolproof.

Serves 6-8

HASTY BLUEBERRY & APRICOT BREAD PUDDING

The easiest dessert ever—a fruit bread pudding served warm—tops off a stress-free meal. Served in a deep dish or bowl, this dessert stands on its own, though a dollop of crème fraîche or fresh whipped cream is an extra treat.

In a large shallow baking dish, arrange EIGHT TO TEN ½-INCH SLICES CHALLAH (brioche, or other similar egg bread works well). Peel and pit 8 RIPE APRICOTS (or 4 peaches or nectarines, or canned apricots), then cut into slices. Place in a large bowl with 3 CUPS BLUEBERRIES. In another bowl mix together: ¾ CUP HONEY, 2-3 TABLESPOONS FRESH LEMON JUICE, and ¼ CUP COINTREAU or other fruit liqueur. Add to fruit and mix to coat. Pour mixture over bread, distributing fruit evenly. Cover tightly with foil and bake approximately 45 minutes in a 350°F oven until fruit is soft. The ripeness of the fruit determines cooking time. Serve warm or at room temperature.

Serves 6 - 8

Candlelight
Dinner for Two

*Adding nutmeg to the pea soup guarantees that your
meal is off to a favorable start. Serve this elegant and simple menu
with warm dinner rolls.*

Shortcut Pea Soup

Wine Poached Salmon with Horseradish Dill Sauce

Endive & Walnut Salad with Walnut Vinaigrette

Wild Rice with Almonds & Raisins

Sliced Peaches with Crème Fraîche & Brown Sugar

SHORTCUT PEA SOUP

This rich and delicately seasoned soup, made quickly in a blender or food processor, will taste as though you spent hours in the kitchen.

Boil 3 CUPS FROZEN PEAS in salted water until tender, according to directions on the package. Drain the peas and place in a blender or food processor. Add ¼ CUP CHICKEN BROTH and purée until smooth. Add 1 CUP HEAVY CREAM, a little at a time. Blend. Pour into a saucepan and stir in ½ TEASPOON SALT, ¼ TEASPOON FRESHLY GROUND BLACK PEPPER, and ½ TEASPOON FRESHLY GRATED NUTMEG. Heat thoroughly but do not boil. Garnish each bowl with a DOLLOP OF SOUR CREAM and serve.

Serves 2

WINE POACHED SALMON WITH HORSERADISH DILL SAUCE

To simplify cleanup, line baking dish with foil and seal fish tightly. The tangy sauce can be made the day before.

Place TWO 6-OUNCE SALMON FILLETS in a small shallow baking dish. Squeeze FRESH LEMON JUICE over fillets. Pour enough DRY WHITE WINE over fish to cover. Place a lid on the baking dish or seal tightly with foil. Bake in a preheated 450°F oven approximately 12 minutes for rare fish, or until cooked to desired doneness. (Check fish frequently to avoid overcooking.) Remove fish from dish, draining off excess wine, and place on dinner plates on a bed of BABY LETTUCE or FRESH PARSLEY. Sprinkle with SALT and FRESHLY GROUND BLACK PEPPER to taste.

HORSERADISH DILL SAUCE

Combine ½ CUP SOUR CREAM, 2 TABLESPOONS HORSERADISH, and 3 TABLESPOONS FRESH CHOPPED DILL. Spoon on top of salmon fillets just before serving. Garnish with a SPRIG OF DILL.

Serves 2

ENDIVE & WALNUT SALAD WITH WALNUT VINAIGRETTE

To ensure crispness, this salad should be put together shortly before serving. To save time, make the dressing in advance and have the other ingredients measured and ready. You may wish to serve it either before or after the main course.

Cut 1 HEAD BELGIAN ENDIVE into julienne. Place in a bowl. Add ½ CUP LARGE WALNUT PIECES. Toss to incorporate walnuts.

COOKING TIP:
For a delicious variation, add sliced ripe pears such as Bartlett or Bosc.

Serves 2

WALNUT VINAIGRETTE DRESSING

Combine 6 TABLESPOONS WALNUT OIL, 3 TABLESPOONS WHITE WINE VINEGAR, 1 TABLESPOON FRESH LEMON JUICE, and SALT to taste. Shake in a jar or whisk to incorporate. Just before serving, drizzle dressing over endive and walnut pieces and toss gently. Arrange salad on individual plates and sprinkle with CRUMBLED BLUE CHEESE.

Serves 2

WILD RICE WITH ALMONDS & RAISINS

What's especially nice about this rice dish is that you can add or subtract ingredients according to the needs of your meal (and your time). It's tasty using just the slivered almonds and chopped cilantro. Serve warm or at room temperature.

Prepare a 12-OUNCE BOX WILD RICE according to directions on package. Run the cooked rice under cold water to stop cooking process, and drain well. Add to rice: ½ CUP CHOPPED TOMATOES, ¼ CUP TOASTED, SLIVERED ALMONDS, ¼ CUP RAISINS, ¼ CUP PITTED BLACK OLIVES, ¼ CUP CHOPPED CILANTRO, and 2 TABLESPOONS FINELY CHOPPED JALAPEÑO PEPPERS. Mix to incorporate. Splash mixture lightly with EXTRA-VIRGIN OLIVE OIL and BALSAMIC VINEGAR to taste. Season with SALT and FRESHLY GROUND BLACK PEPPER and toss.

COOKING TIP:
Add Cold Chicken, Shrimp, or Tuna to leftovers for a delicious lunch. Other savory additions: Scallions, Artichoke Hearts, Shredded Carrots, Currants, Walnuts, or Celery.

Serves 2 with leftovers

SLICED PEACHES WITH CRÈME FRAÎCHE & BROWN SUGAR

Crème Fraîche adds a rich tart taste to fresh fruit. It is extremely simple to prepare but must be made in advance.

Combine equal parts of HEAVY CREAM and SOUR CREAM in a small bowl or jar. Cover and allow to stand 12 to 18 hours at room temperature. Refrigerate. If desired, sweeten with a small amount of SUGAR before serving. Or, better yet, after you top the SLICED PEACHES with Crème Fraîche, sprinkle with BROWN SUGAR and serve immediately.

Serves 2

SUPER SUPPER

No longer is turkey a once-a-year bird! Its tender white meat is the centerpiece of this simple menu—the kind of dish that begs to be passed around a table of friends in a big serving bowl. This meal is perfect with a loaf of fresh whole-grain bread.

Turkey Stew with Bow Tie Pasta

Romaine Lettuce with Lime & Cilantro Dressing

Easy Almond Bars

TURKEY STEW WITH BOW TIE PASTA

Prepare this dish the day before, if you wish. Just be certain the green bell peppers are cut in chunks and still have a bit of crunch left when cooked. Grated Parmesan cheese is a nice accompaniment, and the brinier the black olives, the better! The turkey dish should be served over the hot pasta—either at the table or from the kitchen.

Cut 1½ POUNDS BONELESS TURKEY BREAST into ½- by 2-inch strips. In a large skillet, heat ¼ CUP OLIVE OIL. Cook the turkey strips over moderate heat until browned—approximately 2-3 minutes, stirring constantly. (Depending on the size of your skillet, you may wish to cook the turkey meat in two batches.) Remove with slotted spoon and set aside. In the remaining olive oil, sauté 1 LARGE ONION coarsely chopped, and 2 LARGE GARLIC CLOVES chopped, until browned but not wilted. Add 2 LARGE GREEN BELL PEPPERS chopped into large chunks and continue to sauté. (If the vegetables have begun to stick to the pan, you may wish to add a bit more oil.) Add 2 POUNDS WHOLE RIPE TOMATOES chopped (or two 14-ounce cans whole tomatoes with their juice, breaking up tomatoes in the skillet). Add ¼ CUP KALAMATA-STYLE PITTED BLACK OLIVES, 1 TEASPOON DRIED THYME, 1 TEASPOON DRIED OREGANO, ½ CUP DRY WHITE WINE, SALT and FRESHLY GROUND BLACK PEPPER to taste. Add cooked turkey strips to skillet and heat to boil. Thicken with TOMATO PASTE. Cover and cook for 10-15 minutes.

Serves 6-8

BOW TIE PASTA

Prepare one 16 OUNCE BOX BOW TIE PASTA according to package directions. Drain thoroughly and place in a large bowl. Drizzle with a small amount of EXTRA-VIRGIN OLIVE OIL and toss. Sprinkle with CHOPPED FRESH PARSLEY and FRESHLY GRATED CHEESE such as Parmesan or Romano. Serve in a separate bowl or toss together with Turkey Stew.

COOKING TIP:
Elephant garlic is larger, but more mellow in flavor than regular garlic, so go ahead and substitute one clove of this type for two regular garlic cloves.

Serves 6

ROMAINE LETTUCE WITH
LIME & CILANTRO DRESSING

Wait until just before serving to toss the greens with the dressing.

Combine in a jar: ¼ Cup Vegetable Oil, 3 Tablespoons Fresh Lime Juice, 1 Garlic Clove minced, ½ Cup Coarsely Chopped Fresh Cilantro Leaves (or more according to taste), and Salt and Freshly Ground Black Pepper to taste. Tear 1 Large Head Romaine Lettuce into small pieces and place in a large bowl. Toss with dressing.

Serves 6

Easy Almond Bars

This delicious, crispy bar cookie is mixed in one bowl with little fuss and little muss.

Cream together 2 Cups Sugar and 1½ Sticks Salted Butter. Add 1 Egg, 1 Tablespoon Grated Lemon Rind, 1 Teaspoon Vanilla, 1 Teaspoon Almond Extract and blend. Add ⅛ Teaspoon Salt and 2 Cups All-Purpose Flour, a little at a time, and mix thoroughly. Stir in 1 Cup Slivered Almonds. Press batter into a well-greased 9- by 13-inch baking pan. Bake at 350°F for 30 minutes. Cool on rack for 2 minutes. With a sharp knife, cut into bars and transfer to rack to cool completely. Makes about a dozen bars.

Serves 6 - 8

FANCY BUFFET FOR A DOZEN

The joy of this inviting menu is that it's planned to keep the cook out of the kitchen, even with so many guests to feed and keep happy. With the exception of the potatoes, everything can be made well in advance.

Cajun-Style Meat Loaf with Salsa

Onion Mashed Potatoes

Cool-As-a-Cucumber Salad

Sautéed Zucchini & Yellow Squash

Snappy Apple Crisp

CAJUN-STYLE MEAT LOAF WITH SALSA

This is but one variation of a flavorful meat loaf that has been developed by New York restaurateur Peter Mirabella. It requires only a little more in the preparation time than standard meat loaf, but it can be made the day before and stored in the baking pan, ready to be popped into the oven. The salsa can also be made in advance.

In a large mixing bowl, add 2 POUNDS GROUND BEEF, 3 LARGE EGGS and approximately 20 CRUMBLED SALTINE CRACKERS. Mix lightly. Add ¾ CUP TOMATO JUICE and ¼ CUP HEAVY CREAM. Set aside. Combine the spices in a bowl: 1½ TABLESPOONS EACH of DRY MUSTARD, PAPRIKA, THYME LEAVES, and BASIL; 1 TABLESPOON EACH of GARLIC POWDER and ONION POWDER; ½ TABLESPOON EACH of BLACK PEPPER, WHITE PEPPER, and SALT. Sauté 1 SMALL ONION finely chopped in 3 TABLESPOONS OLIVE OIL until onion is wilted but not browned. Add 2 STALKS CELERY finely chopped and 1 MEDIUM GREEN BELL PEPPER finely chopped. Add spice mixture to vegetables and sauté for 2 minutes. Remove from heat and add to meat mixture. Mix lightly and quickly so as not to overwork. Add 1½ - 2 CUPS UNFLAVORED BREAD CRUMBS to mixture until it holds together. Mold mixture into 2 loaves and place in 2 lightly oiled loaf pans.

Bake at 350°F for 50-60 minutes, or until meat is thoroughly cooked yet still moist.

Serves 6 - 8

SALSA

Combine the following in a bowl: 1 CUP FINELY CHOPPED TOMATOES, and ½ CUP EACH FINELY CHOPPED CELERY, GREEN PEPPER, and RED ONION. Add 1 TABLESPOON WHITE WINE VINEGAR, ½ CUP or more TOMATO JUICE, and DASH OF HOT RED PEPPER SAUCE to taste. Thicken with TOMATO KETCHUP.

COOKING TIP:
To save time, chop the salsa vegetables when you chop the vegetables for the meat loaf. Just remember to use the sweet red onion in the salsa. Also, the meat loaf vegetables should be more finely chopped than those for the salsa.

Serves 12

ONION MASHED POTATOES

The onion adds a little something extra to homemade mashed potatoes.

Peel 12 LARGE BAKING POTATOES. Cut into 2-inch cubes and cook in salted water until tender (approximately 15 minutes). While potatoes are cooking, sauté 1 LARGE SPANISH ONION chopped, in 1 STICK UNSALTED BUTTER. Set aside. When potatoes are tender, drain and immediately place in a large mixing bowl. Add onion mixture, 1 CUP HEAVY CREAM, ¼ CUP CHOPPED PARSLEY, and SALT and FRESHLY GROUND BLACK PEPPER to taste. Whip at high speed with electric mixer or mix by hand. (Potatoes are delicious served lumpy or smooth.)

COOKING TIP:
You can always put mashed potatoes in a deep casserole and reheat in a conventional oven or microwave just before serving.

Serves 6-8

COOL-AS-A-CUCUMBER SALAD

The cucumbers are the perfect complement to a spicy meal! The creamy dressing can be prepared well in advance. In fact, it makes a delicious dip for vegetables, so consider making double the recipe just to have some on hand.

Mix together: 1 CUP SOUR CREAM, 1 CUP MAYONNAISE, ⅓ CUP CHOPPED PARSLEY, 3 TABLESPOONS SNIPPED CHIVES, 1 TABLESPOON WHITE WINE VINEGAR, 1 GARLIC CLOVE crushed, ¼ TEASPOON SALT, and ⅛ TEASPOON GROUND WHITE PEPPER. Refrigerate until ready to use. Peel 8-10 CUCUMBERS and cut in half lengthwise. Scoop out seeds with a spoon. Cut into thick pieces (½ inch). Add enough dressing to coat cucumbers thoroughly. Garnish with FRESH CHIVES.

Serves 12

SAUTÉED ZUCCHINI & YELLOW SQUASH

These colorful vegetables hold up well when cooked in advance and served at room temperature.

Cut 4 ZUCCHINI, 4 YELLOW SQUASH and 1 LARGE SWEET ONION (such as Vidalia) into chunky pieces. In a large skillet, sauté vegetables in just enough OLIVE OIL to keep them from sticking to the pan and cook until soft, but still firm. Add SALT and FRESHLY GROUND BLACK PEPPER to taste.

Serves 12

SNAPPY APPLE CRISP

No recipe collection is complete without this easy, inexpensive dessert. It's a guaranteed crowd pleaser. Make double the recipe for a dozen people and bake in a large shallow baking pan, or divide between two 9- by 9-inch pans. It's delicious served with vanilla ice cream.

In a bowl soak ½ CUP RAISINS in 2 TABLESPOONS BRANDY. Set aside. Mix together 1 CUP FLOUR, 1 CUP ROLLED OATS, 1 TEASPOON BAKING POWDER, and 1½ CUPS DARK BROWN SUGAR. Add ⅔ CUP BUTTER, and cut into mixture with a pastry cutter (or two knives) until crumbly. Core, peel, and slice about 2 POUNDS OF APPLES to layer the bottom of a 9- by 9-inch pan. Sprinkle apples with 1½ TEASPOONS CINNAMON and a PINCH OF NUTMEG. Toss with the RAISINS AND BRANDY. Cover the apple slices with crumb mixture and pat down slightly. Sprinkle with a ½ CUP COARSELY CHOPPED WALNUTS. Bake at 350°F for 25-30 minutes.

Serves 6

MEMORABLE ONE-POT DINNER

This hearty soup, a meal in itself, combines a delicious wine and tomato base, with ample portions of seafood and vegetables. Serve with a mixed green salad dressed in oil, lemon juice, and a sprinkling of fresh herbs. Amaretto cookies go perfectly with the pear dessert.

HEARTY SEAFOOD SOUP

PARMESAN-GARLIC TOASTS

PEARS À L'ORANGE

HEARTY SEAFOOD SOUP

This is a richly flavorful adaptation of a favorite bouillabaisse recipe. The soup base can be prepared in advance, adding the potato cubes and fresh fish shortly before serving. (Just be sure to heat base thoroughly before proceeding with recipe.) Ladle this hearty soup into large bowls at the table and top with sprigs of fresh herbs.

Heat 3 TABLESPOONS OLIVE OIL in large pot over medium heat. Add 1 LARGE ONION chopped, 4 LARGE CLOVES GARLIC minced, 3 LEEKS SLICED ½ INCH THICK, and 4 MEDIUM CARROTS chopped. Cook, stirring, until vegetables begin to wilt. Add following ingredients: ONE 28-OUNCE CAN plus ONE 14-OUNCE CAN WHOLE TOMATOES with JUICE (crush them slightly as you add), 1 CUP DRY WHITE WINE, 2 CUPS CHICKEN BROTH, 1 TEASPOON OREGANO LEAVES, ½ TEASPOON SUGAR, ¼ TEASPOON RED PEPPER FLAKES, 4 SPRIGS FRESH THYME (or 2 TEASPOONS DRIED THYME), and 1 BAY LEAF. Cover and simmer 20 minutes. Add 3 CUPS PEELED POTATOES cut into small bite-sized cubes. Continue to simmer for another 10 minutes.

Add 1½ Pounds of White-Fleshed, Non-Oily Fish (Halibut, Cod, Tile, Monkfish, or Haddock) cut into cubes, ½ Pound Large Shrimp cleaned and deveined, and ½ Pound Scallops. (You may also use fresh Mussels, Clams or Lobster.) Cover and simmer for 10 to 15 minutes more, or until fish is just cooked through. Check seasoning before serving. Add Salt, if necessary, and Freshly Ground Black Pepper to taste. Garnish each serving with Chopped Fresh Dill and Parsley.

Cooking Tip:

If you wish to substitute fresh fish stock for the chicken broth, use Heads and Tails from Fish, placing them in a large saucepan, covered with 6 Cups Water. Add 1 Bay Leaf, 10 Whole Peppercorns and 1 Tablespoon Salt. Bring to a boil, cover, and lower heat; summer for 1 hour. Strain. Leftover stock may be frozen for future use.

Serves 6 - 8

PARMESAN-GARLIC TOASTS

These are delicious served at room temperature, but at their best right from the broiler. This recipe works well with day-old French or Italian bread.

Slice 1 LARGE LOAF OF FRENCH BREAD on the diagonal and place slices on a broiler tray or baking sheet. Crush 5 GARLIC CLOVES and place in bowl with ¼ CUP EXTRA-VIRGIN OLIVE OIL. Brush oil mixture lightly onto both sides of the bread. Sprinkle both sides with FRESHLY GRATED PARMESAN CHEESE. Place under a preheated broiler. As soon as bread turns golden brown on one side, turn and brown the other side. Place on paper towels to drain excess oil before serving.

Serves 6-8

PEARS À L'ORANGE

This dessert provides a light and tangy finale and it can be served alone or with whipped cream.

Peel 6-8 FIRM, RIPE PEARS (Bartlett are excellent), quarter, and remove cores. Place in a baking dish. In a saucepan, combine 1¼ CUPS FRESH ORANGE JUICE, ½ CUP HONEY, 3 TABLESPOONS COINTREAU, 2 TABLESPOONS FRESH LEMON JUICE, 1 TABLESPOON FRESHLY GRATED GINGER, 1 CINNAMON STICK (about 3 inches long), and 8 WHOLE CLOVES. Bring to boil. Pour mixture over pears. Cover and bake at 350°F for 20-25 minutes. Remove cover and continue cooking 5-10 minutes more, or until just tender. Cooking time will vary, depending on ripeness of pears, so test pears after 20 minutes. Transfer to serving dishes; strain sauce and spoon over pears. Serve warm or at room temperature.

COOKING TIP:
If you use prepared chopped ginger, it is sometimes stronger than fresh ginger and you may wish to adjust the amount accordingly.

Serves 6-8

DAY-BEFORE DINNER

This menu is especially suited to a busy schedule as everything can be done either the day before, or early on the day of the dinner. Serve with hot biscuits and creamery butter.

FANCY GLAZED BAKED HAM

COUNTRY INN HOT FRUIT COMPOTE

VEGETARIAN PASTA SALAD

OLD-FASHIONED GINGERBREAD

FANCY GLAZED BAKED HAM

An old standby and always popular with guests, this ham takes only minutes to dress up and show off.

Place a 4 TO 5-POUND PRECOOKED HAM in a large baking pan and score the top. Insert WHOLE CLOVES at each cross. Brush ham with ¼ CUP DIJON MUSTARD. Sprinkle with 1 CUP DARK BROWN SUGAR, pressing the sugar lightly into the surface. Pour 3 CUPS APPLE JUICE into the bottom of the pan. Bake at 350°F for 1 hour or until heated through, basting once or twice after sugar mixture has formed a crust (overbasting will melt the crust). Place ham on a serving platter and garnish with LETTUCE LEAVES and circles cut from 2 ORANGES sliced. Slice ham thinly and serve.

COOKING TIP:
If you have the time, make a sauce for the ham: Place pan Juices from the ham in small saucepan; spoon off fat.
Add ¼ Cup Raisins and bring to a boil. Thicken with 2 Tablespoons Cornstarch mixed with
¼ Cup Cold Water. Sauce looks especially inviting served hot in a small glass pitcher.

Serves 8

COUNTRY INN HOT FRUIT COMPOTE

The ham's perfect complement!

Pour ONE 35-OUNCE JAR APPLESAUCE into deep baking dish. Add: 3 CUPS MIXED DRIED FRUIT (prunes, apricots, raisins, and cranberries are especially suitable), ¼ CUP COINTREAU or GRAND MARNIER, ONE 8-OUNCE CAN CRUSHED PINEAPPLE WITH JUICE, ¼ CUP BROWN SUGAR, 2 TABLESPOONS FRESHLY GRATED LEMON PEEL, and JUICE OF 1 LEMON. Mix to incorporate.

Add the spices: 1 TEASPOON CINNAMON, ½ TEASPOON GROUND GINGER, ¼ TEASPOON GROUND ALLSPICE, and ⅛ TEASPOON GROUND CLOVES. Cook, covered, in 350°F oven for 1 hour. Stir and cook uncovered for 1 hour more at 300°F, or until fruit is soft and spices are pungent. Serve hot.

Serves 6 - 8

VEGETARIAN PASTA SALAD

This pasta salad has a number of tasty variations. Adjust vegetables according to preference and seasonal offerings.

Prepare half a 16-OUNCE BOX of your favorite PASTA (such as fusilli or small shells) according to the directions on the package. Rinse under cold water to stop cooking; drain, and place in large bowl. Add to pasta: 1 MEDIUM RED ONION finely chopped, 1 MEDIUM ZUCCHINI coarsely chopped, 1 RED BELL PEPPER cut into thin strips, 2-3 TOMATOES cut into small wedges, ⅓ CUP TOASTED PINE NUTS, ¼ CUP CHOPPED FRESH PARSLEY, 1 TABLESPOON SNIPPED FRESH CHIVES, and 2 TEASPOONS CAPERS. Prepare dressing by whisking the following ingredients together or shaking in a covered jar: ½ CUP EXTRA-VIRGIN OLIVE OIL, ½ CUP CANOLA OIL, ⅓ CUP RED WINE VINEGAR, 2 TABLESPOONS DIJON MUSTARD, 1 TABLESPOON CHOPPED FRESH BASIL, and SALT and FRESHLY GROUND BLACK PEPPER to taste. Add dressing to pasta mix and toss gently. Cover and chill at least 1 hour before serving.

COOKING TIP:
Variations to this salad include: Cucumber, Raisins, Sharp Cheddar Cheese, Mozzarella Cheese, Scallion, Green Bell Pepper, Walnuts, and Shredded Carrots.

Serves 8

OLD-FASHIONED GINGERBREAD

Never underestimate the popularity of homemade gingerbread, an all-American favorite. This one goes together quickly, is moist and spicy, and can be prepared the day before.

With an electric mixer, blend together 2 CUPS SUGAR and 6 EGGS. Add 2 CUPS VEGETABLE OIL, 2 CUPS DARK MOLASSES, 1 TEASPOON VANILLA, 1 TABLESPOON each of GROUND CLOVES, GROUND GINGER, and CINNAMON. Mix until smooth. Dissolve 1 TABLESPOON plus 1 TEASPOON BAKING SODA in 4 TABLESPOONS HOT WATER. Add to creamed mixture. Gradually add 4½ CUPS ALL-PURPOSE FLOUR, beating to incorporate well. Add 2 CUPS BOILING WATER, continuing to beat until smooth. Pour batter into well-greased 13- by 13-inch cake pan. Bake at 350°F for 45 minutes, checking for doneness before removing from oven. Cool in oven before cutting. Dust with POWDERED SUGAR before serving.

COOKING TIP:
It saves time to use a stationary electric mixer. Assemble the ingredients ahead of time and, with the mixer running, simply add the ingredients in sequence, scraping the sides of the bowl after additions.

Serves 8

BOARDINGHOUSE REACH

These are updated recipes from times past where third helpings and elbows on the table were always permitted. Serve with hot biscuits or corn bread with plenty of relishes and preserves on the side. In a time pinch, this menu is more than complete without the corn pudding. If time allows, you won't be sorry you went to the extra trouble.

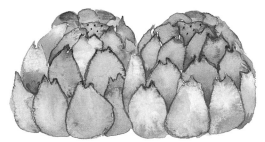

OVEN-FRIED SESAME CHICKEN

BROWN SUGAR BAKED BEANS

HONEY MINT SLAW

AUNT MINNIE'S CORN PUDDING

EASY-AS-PIE PECAN PIE

OVEN-FRIED SESAME CHICKEN

The crispness of fried chicken and the tastiness of sesame are an unbeatable combination. You may wish to toast some sesame seeds in advance—spread them on a baking sheet in a 350°F oven and toast 5-8 minutes until golden brown, shaking several times.

Combine the following ingredients in a shallow dish or pan: 1 CUP TOASTED SESAME SEEDS, 1 CUP FLOUR, 2 TABLESPOONS SALT, 2 TABLESPOONS GARLIC POWDER, and 2 TABLESPOONS ONION POWDER. Using paper towels, pat dry 14-18 PIECES CUT-UP CHICKEN, brush well with SESAME SEED MIXTURE and MELTED BUTTER. Place in pan. Coat each piece of chicken well. Place chicken pieces on a well-greased large baking pan. Spray tops of chicken lightly with COOKING OIL, or brush with MELTED BUTTER. Bake in a hot oven (400° F) for approximately 45 minutes to 1 hour, or until juices run clear when chicken is pierced with a fork.

BROWN SUGAR BAKED BEANS

This recipe gives you the heavenly taste of homemade baked beans, but saves you time by using cooked beans from a can. Prepared (but not baked) the night before, the brown sugar will marry with the spicy barbecue sauce.

Add the following ingredients in a large baking dish: FOUR 15-OUNCE CANS PINTO BEANS drained of their juices, 1 CUP SPICY BARBECUE SAUCE, 1 CUP DARK BROWN SUGAR, ½ CUP KETCHUP, 1 SMALL ONION chopped, 2 TABLESPOONS DIJON MUSTARD, 1 TEASPOON SALT, and ½ TEASPOON FRESHLY GROUND BLACK PEPPER. Bake, covered, in a 325°F oven for approximately 1 hour; uncover and bake for an additional hour until the sauce thickens.

HONEY MINT SLAW

Be sure to make plenty! The honey and mint on crunchy cabbage is a favorite that always disappears quickly. Prepare in the morning and refrigerate until 30 minutes before serving.

In large bowl, combine 1 LARGE HEAD CABBAGE (approximately 3 pounds) trimmed and shredded, and 1 LARGE SWEET ONION (such as Vidalia) chopped. In saucepan, combine 1 CUP HONEY, 1 CUP APPLE CIDER VINEGAR, and 1 CUP VEGETABLE OIL. Bring to a boil, stirring to dissolve honey. Allow to cool for 5 minutes. Pour honey mixture over slaw. Toss to mix. Add 4 TEASPOONS CHOPPED FRESH MINT (or more, to taste). Mix well. Cool and refrigerate. Allow to sit at room temperature for 30 minutes before serving. Garnish with SPRIGS OF MINT.

Serves 8

AUNT MINNIE'S CORN PUDDING

The recipe for this tasty corn pudding—a fitting tribute to someone's Aunt Minnie—is a simple one, and it should be prepared shortly before the meal and served piping hot.

Drain 2 CUPS (ONE 16-OUNCE CAN) CORN, setting aside 1 cup. Combine 1 CUP CORN, 1 STICK MELTED BUTTER, 2 CUPS SOUR CREAM, ½ CUP YELLOW CORNMEAL, 2 EGGS, and 1 TEASPOON SALT. Purée mixture in food processor. Place in a large bowl and fold in 2 CUPS GRATED JACK CHEESE, ONE 4-OUNCE CAN DICED GREEN CHILIES drained, and the remaining CORN. Bake in a buttered 9- by 13-inch glass baking dish at 375°F for approximately 40 minutes.

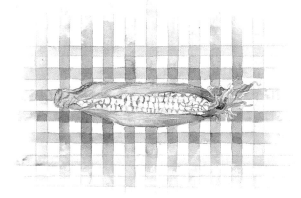

Serves 8

E A S Y - A S - P I E P E C A N P I E

It's sweet, but not too sweet; rich, but who cares when company is coming? Use a frozen pastry shell if time doesn't allow making one from scratch. Serve warm with vanilla ice cream.

Mix together ½ CUP SUGAR and 2 TABLESPOONS MELTED BUTTER. Add 3 LARGE EGGS beaten. Mix well. Add 2 TABLESPOONS ALL-PURPOSE FLOUR and continue mixing. Add 1 CUP LIGHT CORN SYRUP and 1 TEASPOON VANILLA. Beat mixture for 30 seconds. Add 1½ CUPS WHOLE PECANS, stirring in by hand. Pour mixture into UNBAKED 9-INCH PASTRY SHELL. Bake at 375°F for 40-45 minutes. Makes one 9-inch pie.

Serves 6 - 8

SUNDAY NIGHT CASUAL

Serve this appealing pasta dish with a crusty peasant bread. The salad adds color and balance. This simple menu brings the weekend to a most pleasurable conclusion.

Baked Orzo with Mushrooms & Parmesan

Asparagus, Endive & Radicchio Salad

Sweet & Tart Fruit

BAKED ORZO WITH
MUSHROOMS & PARMESAN

Orzo is a versatile rice-shaped pasta that has been much neglected. This recipe combines it with shiitake mushrooms and Parmesan cheese for a texture and a flavor that guests will not soon forget.

Cook 1 POUND ORZO in boiling salted water until al dente. Drain, rinse under cold water, and set aside. Add ¼ CUP OLIVE OIL to large deep skillet. Over medium heat sauté until just wilted: 1 MEDIUM RED ONION sliced and 2 GARLIC CLOVES chopped. Add ⅓ POUND BUTTON MUSHROOMS sliced and ⅓ POUND SHIITAKE MUSHROOMS sliced. Continue to sauté for another 2-3 minutes. Add 2 TABLESPOONS ALL-PURPOSE FLOUR to pan and stir to incorporate. While stirring, slowly add ½ CUP CHICKEN STOCK. Cook for 1 minute. Add 2 TEASPOONS SALT and 1 TEASPOON FRESHLY GROUND BLACK PEPPER. Blend. Remove skillet from flame. Add the cooked

orzo, 1 Cup Freshly Grated Parmesan Cheese, and ½ Cup Fresh Parsley chopped, and stir. Sprinkle top with Grated Parmesan, Seasoned Bread Crumbs, and Fresh Chopped Parsley. Bake in 350°F oven for 30 minutes.

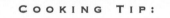

COOKING TIP:
If you cannot locate shiitake mushrooms, use all domestic mushrooms.
You may also substitute Romano cheese for the Parmesan.

Serves 6

ASPARAGUS, ENDIVE & RADICCHIO SALAD

Simply dressed, the natural flavors of this colorful vegetable salad shine through. This salad can be prepared several hours before the meal and served at room temperature or refrigerated until 30 minutes before the meal is served.

Discard the tough ends of 2 POUNDS FRESH ASPARAGUS. Cut asparagus on the bias into 2- and 3-inch–long spears. Blanch for approximately 1 minute in boiling water, depending on the thickness of the asparagus. Remove from heat, drain, and run under very cold water immediately to stop cooking. (Asparagus should be crisp.) Place in a bowl with 1 LARGE HEAD BELGIAN ENDIVE cut into strips and 1 LARGE HEAD RADICCHIO cut into strips. Add ½ CUP EXTRA-VIRGIN OLIVE OIL, 1 TEASPOON SALT, and 1 TEASPOON FRESHLY GROUND BLACK PEPPER. Squeeze the JUICE OF ½ LEMON over vegetables and toss thoroughly. Toss again before serving.

Serves 6

S W E E T & T A R T F R U I T

Slice 4 Cups Seasonal Fruit (peaches, strawberries, orange slices, melon, or a combination) in a bowl. Mix together 3 Parts Honey to 2 Parts Sherry Vinegar. Add to fruit and gently toss. Serve fruit alone or over Sorbet or Ice Cream. Garnish with Sprig of Mint.

Serves 6

Alfresco Buffet

This simple dinner with a Southwestern accent offers a variety of delectable flavors, bright colors, and healthy combinations. Everything short of grilling the fish can be done in advance, leaving the hosts free to be guests at their own party. Serve with warm pita bread.

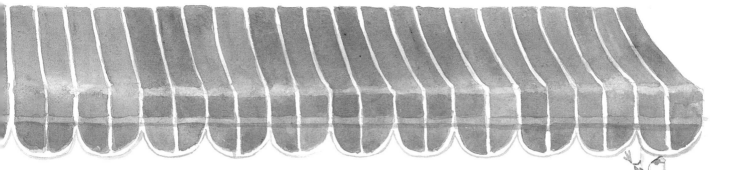

GRILLED SWORDFISH WITH GARLIC BUTTER

CORN & BLACK BEAN SALAD WITH CILANTRO

SLICED NEW POTATOES IN WHITE WINE

BELOVED BROWNIES

GRILLED SWORDFISH WITH GARLIC BUTTER

It takes the pressure off the cook if there's a handy grill in the yard or on the deck or terrace. Failing that, an iron grill pan does the trick. Grilled food is appreciated, indoors and out.

Marinate SIX 6 TO 8-OUNCE SWORDFISH STEAKS for several hours before grilling in 4 TABLESPOONS OLIVE OIL, 2 TABLESPOONS FRESH LIME JUICE, SALT and FRESHLY GROUND BLACK PEPPER to taste.

To prepare garlic butter, combine 1 STICK BUTTER softened, 4 GARLIC CLOVES finely chopped, 1 TABLESPOON FRESH LIME JUICE, and 2 TABLESPOONS FINELY CHOPPED FRESH PARSLEY. Refrigerate until firm.

Grill fish to taste. Top with about 1 TABLESPOON GARLIC BUTTER and a SPRIG OF PARSLEY just before serving.

Serves 6

CORN & BLACK BEAN SALAD
WITH CILANTRO

The corn and beans in this recipe can be combined ahead of time with the tomatoes, but the cilantro and dressing should be put on shortly before serving for maximum freshness and flavor.

Combine in bowl: TWO 15-OUNCE CANS BLACK BEANS drained with ONE 11-OUNCE CAN VACUUM-PACKED WHOLE CORN drained.

Add 3 MEDIUM TOMATOES chopped, 1 RED (or GREEN) BELL PEPPER chopped, and 1 SMALL RED ONION chopped. Toss to combine.

Sprinkle with ½ CUP CHOPPED FRESH CILANTRO, ¼ CUP OLIVE OIL, ¼ CUP BALSAMIC VINEGAR, and SALT and FRESHLY GROUND BLACK PEPPER to taste. Toss before serving.

Serves 6

SLICED NEW POTATOES
IN WHITE WINE

The secret of this dish is to not overcook the potatoes. If you have a microwave, the entire dish can be prepared well in advance and warmed just before serving.

Place 2 POUNDS SMALL NEW POTATOES in a saucepan with cold water to cover. Bring to a boil and cook until potatoes are cooked but still very firm (about 15 minutes).

Drain potatoes and peel under cold water. Slice thinly and place in a bowl. Pour ½ CUP DRY WHITE WINE and ½ CUP EXTRA-VIRGIN OLIVE OIL over potatoes. Add MINCED GARLIC to taste. Sprinkle with SALT, FRESHLY GROUND BLACK PEPPER, and a generous amount of FRESH THYME. Toss. Place mixture in a serving dish and serve warm.

Serves 6

BELOVED BROWNIES

These rich, moist brownies can be mixed in one bowl. They keep well overnight and are deliciously decadent served with a scoop of vanilla or coffee ice cream.

Melt 4 OUNCES UNSWEETENED CHOCOLATE and 1 CUP UNSALTED BUTTER in large saucepan. Set aside. Combine in bowl: 2 CUPS SUGAR, 4 LARGE EGGS lightly beaten, ½ TEASPOON VANILLA, and ½ TEASPOON SALT. Beat to incorporate. Beat in chocolate and butter mixture. Add 1 CUP ALL-PURPOSE FLOUR and continue beating for 1 minute. Fold in 1 CUP COARSELY CHOPPED PECANS (or WALNUTS). Pour batter into a well-greased 9- by 13-inch baking pan. Bake for 20-25 minutes in 350°F oven. Do not overbake. Cool before cutting.

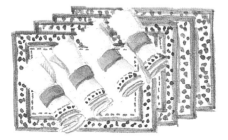

Makes about a dozen brownies

SIT-DOWN ELEGANCE

This wonderful and delicious meal is amazingly stress-free. Your guests won't believe how simple the creamy mushroom sauce is because it looks and tastes truly gourmet. Make the chocolate sauce well in advance, but keep it hidden in the back of the refrigerator.

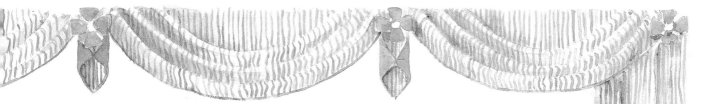

Orange & Fennel Salad with Sage

Filet of Beef with Piquant Mushroom Sauce

Fancy Poppy-Seed Rice

Baked Tomatoes with Thyme

Vanilla Ice Cream with Spicy Chocolate Sauce

ORANGE & FENNEL SALAD WITH SAGE

The slightly licorice taste of fennel and the sweetness of the sliced oranges and the red onions is a refreshing combination.

Trim fronts and remove the cores from 3-4 BULBS OF FENNEL (depending on size) and slice into very thin slices. Peel 2 MEDIUM RED ONIONS. Cut in half lengthwise and slice thinly. Peel 4 LARGE SEEDLESS NAVEL ORANGES. Cut in half lengthwise and slice. Cut the leaves from 2 BUNCHES FRESH SAGE. Roll up bunches of the leaves together tightly and slice crosswise to make

Serves 6

thin strips. Just before serving, combine fennel, onion, oranges, and sage in a large bowl. Add EXTRA-VIRGIN OLIVE OIL and then BALSAMIC VINEGAR. Toss. Season with SALT and FRESHLY GROUND BLACK PEPPER to taste. Toss and serve immediately.

COOKING TIP:
Chiffonade is the term used for a leafy vegetable or fresh herb that has been finely shredded or sliced.

Serves 6-8

FILET OF BEEF WITH PIQUANT MUSHROOM SAUCE

Grill or roast a whole tenderloin of beef according to desired doneness, or serve individual grilled slices of filet mignon. Whichever you choose, the mushroom sauce adds to the natural flavor of the meat. If you cannot locate a fine prepared *diable* sauce, a gourmet-style steak sauce may be substituted. The Piquant Cream Sauce may be served over the meat and sprinkled with chopped fresh parsley. Or, if you wish, serve on the side.

Over medium heat, sauté 6-8 THINLY SLICED MUSHROOMS (shiitake are preferred). In another saucepan combine 1½ CUPS GOURMET-STYLE STEAK SAUCE and 1 CUP HEAVY CREAM. Add mushrooms and heat, stirring, until combined. Serve hot.

COOKING TIP:
Using an oil spray coats the pan just enough to sauté the mushrooms quickly.

Serves 6-8

FANCY POPPY-SEED RICE

There are dozens of simple ways to dress up plain white rice. This is one of them.

Prepare 2 CUPS LONG-GRAIN WHITE RICE according to package directions. While the rice is cooking, sauté ½ CUP ONION minced in 3 TABLESPOONS BUTTER until golden brown. Combine hot cooked rice with sautéed onion and 3 TABLESPOONS POPPY-SEEDS. Add SALT to taste and serve hot.

Serves 6

BAKED TOMATOES WITH THYME

As the garlic and rosemary fill the kitchen with good smells, you will earn high marks on your simple tomato dish before dinner is served.

Cut 8 PLUM TOMATOES in half lengthwise. Place them cut side down in a small baking dish that has been greased lightly with OLIVE OIL. Sprinkle tomatoes with SALT, FRESHLY GROUND BLACK PEPPER, GARLIC SALT, and DRIED ROSEMARY. Drizzle lightly with OLIVE OIL. Bake in a preheated 450°F oven for 5-8 minutes. Remove from oven and sprinkle with CHOPPED FRESH PARSLEY.

Serves 6

VANILLA ICE CREAM WITH SPICY CHOCOLATE SAUCE

This recipe makes about 2 cups of chocolate sauce. If there's any left over, it stores well in the refrigerator for about 2 weeks.

Melt 5 SQUARES UNSWEETENED CHOCOLATE and 2 TABLESPOONS BUTTER in saucepan, stirring to prevent burning. In separate bowl, combine 2 CUPS SUGAR, 2 TEASPOONS CORNSTARCH, A PINCH OF SALT, 1 TEASPOON GROUND ALLSPICE, and 1 TEASPOON GROUND CINNAMON. Add mixture to melted chocolate and butter. Blend. Stir in 1½ CUPS BOILING WATER. Simmer 3 minutes or until sauce has thickened. Cool and add 2 TEASPOONS VANILLA. Chill slightly before serving over ice cream or pound cake (or both).

Serves 6-8

KID-FRIENDLY
PANTRY IMPROMPTU

Every cook should have a pantry stocked with a few items that can become tasty spur-of-the-moment meals. Most of the ingredients in this no-panic menu are probably waiting on a shelf or in your refrigerator. This meal is great for kids when the dinner party is a family affair.

PASTA WITH PESTO

EVERYTHING CHOPPED SALAD WITH BALSAMIC VINAIGRETTE

DECADENT TOFFEE BARS

PASTA WITH PESTO

Keep a container or two of pesto sauce in your freezer for unexpected company. Serve over your favorite hot pasta. Sprinkle with grated parmesan or romano cheese.

Cook a 1-POUND BOX OF PASTA (such as angel hair or linguini) according to package directions. Toss with PESTO SAUCE and FRESHLY GRATED PARMESAN CHEESE. Add SALT and FRESHLY GROUND BLACK PEPPER to taste. Serve hot.

EVERYTHING CHOPPED SALAD WITH BALSAMIC VINAIGRETTE

You will be amazed at the colorful and tasty salad you can put together from the vegetables in your refrigerator, supplemented with canned green beans, peas, or carrots.

Coarsely chop 4 CUPS of your favorite VEGETABLES. In a jar, combine ¼ CUP EXTRA-VIRGIN OLIVE OIL, ¼ CUP CANOLA OIL, ¼ CUP PLUS 1 TABLESPOON BALSAMIC VINEGAR, 1 TABLESPOON DIJON MUSTARD, 1 GARLIC CLOVE crushed, 1 TEASPOON DRIED OREGANO, and SALT and FRESHLY GROUND BLACK PEPPER to taste. Shake well. Pour over chopped vegetables and toss well.

Serves 4-6

DECADENT TOFFEE BARS

This sweet and gooey graham cracker and chocolate dessert—more candy than cookie—will remind you of your childhood. It's a kid-friendly dessert to make and to demolish. Store extras in the refrigerator.

Line a 9- by 13-inch baking pan with foil and grease it well with BUTTER. Cover bottom of pan with two layers of GRAHAM CRACKERS (ABOUT 30-36 SQUARE CRACKERS), breaking crackers, if necessary, to make them fit flat. In a saucepan, combine 1 CUP BROWN SUGAR and 2 STICKS UNSALTED BUTTER and melt; stirring. Stir in 1 TEASPOON VANILLA. Pour melted mixture over graham crackers. Bake in 400°F oven for 5 minutes. Remove and immediately sprinkle with 1 CUP SEMISWEET CHOCOLATE CHIPS. As soon as the chips have melted, spread over surface of graham crackers with spatula. Sprinkle with ½ CUP CHOPPED PECANS or WALNUTS. Gently press nuts into chocolate. Chill in baking pan for 30 minutes to 1 hour. When ready to serve, break into small cookie-sized pieces.

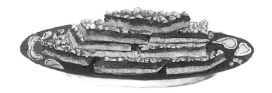

Serves 4-6